Should There Be

A Persuasive Text

Written by Tony Stead

with Judy Ballester and her fourth-grade class

For all of the animals in the world who are diseased,
are used for entertainment purposes, or are endangered,
we hope this book makes a difference.

Acknowledgments

The authors would like to thank the following people for their assistance and support—Nancy Birson, Staff Developer at District 10; Lenore Mironchik, Children's Librarian at Hillcrest Library; Pat Nevins, School Librarian at P.S. 148; our parents; our principal, Mr. Sal Romano, and the staff at P.S. 148; Gina Shaw at Mondo Publishing.

Photo Credits

Copyright © by Richard and Jacob Hutchings:
Cover, p. 1, p. 3, p. 5, p. 7 (top), p. 8 (left), p. 9, p. 10, p. 11, p. 13 (top photos),
p. 14 (bottom), p. 15 (top photos), p. 17 (top), p. 19 (top photos), p. 21 (all photos),
p. 23 (top), p. 25 (both photos), p. 27, p. 28, p. 29, p. 30.

Copyright © by ANIMALS ANIMALS
p. 7 (bottom) © George Bernard, p. 8 (right) © Stouffer Productions, Ltd.,
p. 11 (bottom) © Richard Kolar, p. 12 (left) © Mickey Gibson, p. 12 (right) © Joanne F. Huemoeller,
p. 13 (bottom) © Lynn Stone, p. 14 (top) © Michael Dick, p. 14 (middle) © Fred Whitehead,
p. 15 (bottom) © John Chellman, p. 16 (left) © William B. Robinson, p. 16 (right) © David Barron,
p. 17 (bottom) © James Watt, p. 18 (left) © Joe McDonald, p. 18 (right) © R. Cannon,
p. 19 (bottom) © M. Colbeck, p. 20 (left) © Ken Cole, p. 20 (right) © John Nees,
p. 23 (bottom) © Norbert Rosing, p. 24 © Terry G. Murphy, p. 26 © Stewart D. Halperin

Zooasaurus illustration copyright © by Marilyn Zucker

Text copyright © by Tony Stead

For information contact:
MONDO Publishing
980 Avenue of the Americas, New York, NY 10018
Visit our website at www.mondopub.com
Printed in China
Regent Publishing Services, Guandong, Province, ID# 12497

Designed by Jean Cohn
Photoshop collage of question mark by Steven Umansky
ISBN 978-1-57255-817-5

Contents

Introduction

What Is a Zoo?

This book focuses on the question, *Should animals be kept in zoos?* When we began researching this topic, the first thing we had to do was define the word *zoo*. This is our definition.

A zoo is a public place where living animals are kept in some type of **enclosure**. For **aquatic** animals, a zoo can be an **aquarium**. For the purposes of this book, we are including aquariums as zoos. We also feel that wildlife centers, safari parks, and refuge centers can be thought of as zoos.

However, we have chosen not to include circuses because we think circuses are different from zoos. A circus uses animals exclusively to entertain people. A zoo provides animal entertainment for people as only *part* of its purpose.

What Is a Persuasive Text?

This book is a persuasive text. We've written our opinions about a topic and supported them with facts. We have found these facts on the Internet, in newspaper and magazine articles, on a field trip, and in books. We have used all of the facts to try to persuade, or convince, you to feel the same way we do.

Some of us are going to try to convince you that zoos are necessary. We will argue that zoos help prevent **extinction,** provide protection and care for animals, and help us learn more about animals and their **habitats**.

Others of us are going to try to persuade you that animals should not be confined to zoos. We will argue that such **confinement** can cause death, disease, and a mental illness known as **zoochosis**. We will also argue that it is not natural to confine animals, and that zoos do not always provide protection and care.

At the end of the book, we will show you the steps we used to write this persuasive text in case you want to write your own.

Should Animals Be Kept in Zoos? You Make the Decision.

At the end of each argument in this book, you will see a cartoon character. This is Zooasaurus.

If Zooasaurus is holding up a green flag, it means this is an argument *for* zoos. If Zooasaurus is holding up a red flag, it means this is an argument *against* zoos. After you read each argument, you will need to decide how convincing the argument was.

Give the argument 3 points if you think it was a very strong one. Give the argument 2 points if you think it was adequate, and 1 point if you think it was poor. Keep a piece of paper and a pencil handy as you read through the book so that you can record your points. At the end of the book, tally up all the points that were in favor of having zoos; then tally up all those against having zoos. This will help you decide how effective we were at convincing you whether or not animals should be kept in zoos. Happy reading!

Extinction and Endangered Animals

"Zoos must intervene, to help prevent extinction."—RONNY CALLE

Our world is losing wildlife at an alarming rate. Scientists estimate that 50,000 **species** of plants and animals are doomed to extinction each year—that's about six an hour. From toads to tigers, animals everywhere are in a fight for their future. Who's to blame? We are. The global human population of around seven billion is increasing by about 85 million each year. As our species takes over wildlife habitats, other species are threatened, and in many cases, lost. As the naturalist William Beebe wrote in 1906, "When the last individual of a race of living things breathes no more, another heaven and earth must pass before such one can be again."

dodo bird

Dodo birds roamed our earth hundreds of years ago, but now they are extinct—gone forever! Dodos were fat birds with tiny wings. They were unable to fly. In the late 1500s, people from Europe came to the islands where dodos lived. They found the dodos tasty and easy to catch. In less than 100 years, dodos became extinct. People were shocked. How could an entire species be wiped out in such a short period of time? It was truly unbelievable!

Animals like the Atlas bear were not killed primarily by people. Their population slowly diminished as their habitat began to disappear. Atlas bears lived in the forests of North Africa. These forests had an abundance of trees. People started cutting down the trees. The Atlas bears were losing their habitat quickly! Over time, the land became a desert. By the late 1800s, these bears became extinct as well.

passenger pigeon

tombstone listing extinct animals of the 1500s

Another example is the passenger pigeon. These birds migrated in flocks, so you would think they would be safe. Wrong! Humans started shooting these pigeons for pure enjoyment. Others sold the birds for food. The last living passenger pigeon was seen in September 1914.

Has our species, the human race, ever been hunted for food? I can't even begin to think what this would feel like. Imagine going to bed each evening and wondering if you would see the next sunrise. Unfortunately, if you were a Rodriquez greater tortoise, you *would* understand. These tortoises were the main meal for the French and the English navies. Ships would stop at the Rodriquez Islands to round up tortoises before embarking on a long voyage. The tortoise population began to shrink. Laws were passed about the number of tortoises the people onboard the ships could take with them. However, no one obeyed these laws. Didn't these people realize that if they kept eating these animals at such a fast pace, there wouldn't be any left? Apparently not. By 1795, the Rodriquez greater tortoises were gone forever!

tombstone listing endangered animals of the 1900s

Although there is no hope left for these animals, there is a lot we can do for so many other animals whose existence is in danger. If your mom or dad or your best friend was very ill, wouldn't you want to help? Of course you would. We need to aid those animals who are in danger of becoming extinct, and zoos are our best answer.

Animals in the wild are never free from predators, disease, loss of their natural habitats, and starvation. A good zoo, however, can provide food, shelter, and preservation of wildlife.

"Imagine endangered animals out in the wild, all alone."—GUCCI ATEHONTUA

Animals that live in very small numbers and are in danger of disappearing forever are called **endangered**. People cause three main types of danger to animals. First, animals are overhunted for food, for their hides, or just for sport. Second, animals are losing their natural habitats. People chop down trees for lumber. They clear fields to plant crops, and they fill swamps to build towns and highways. Third, animal habitats are becoming unhealthy due to pollution. Oil spills pollute the water, harming aquatic animals. The spraying of pesticides by farmers causes harm to other animals.

Imagine never seeing a bird fly in the sky or never hearing a bee buzzing in an energetic search for pollen. Imagine never seeing a caterpillar transform into a glorious butterfly. Hard to believe, isn't it? You know that if you break the **food chain,** everything slowly ceases to exist. That means people will die as well.

There are many animals throughout the world, like the giant panda, the tiger, and the orangutan, that are in great danger. How can we save our wildlife? We can ask zoos to help.

Zoochosis

"It was the sadness in their eyes that has continued to haunt us."
—STEPHANIE SANTANA AND SHAUWN LUKOSE

Keep animals in zoos! We don't think so. There is documented research that many animals removed from their natural habitat and kept in **captivity** have developed a kind of mental illness known as zoochosis.

Animals with this disease often pace back and forth, twist their necks, bob their heads up and down, turn in never-ending circles, and even tear holes in their own skin. Can you imagine being so miserable that you would want to inflict harm on yourself?

pacing tiger

Once, when we visited a zoo, we noticed that some of the animals kept in cages were grabbing onto the bars and shaking them. If you could have looked into these animals' eyes like we did, you would have seen deep sadness. It is this sadness that continues to haunt us to this day.

It has been documented that Junior, a killer whale, was removed from his natural habitat in Iceland and placed in a tank in Niagara Falls. He died four years later, deprived of outside air, sunlight, and companionship.

Junior is not alone. There are many aquatic animals that are taken from their natural habitats and placed in water tanks in

beluga whales

orca

aquariums around the world. These animals are separated from their families and are forced to live in groups that are nothing like their own families. As though that isn't enough, animals like whales and dolphins, who are accustomed to swimming up to 100 miles in one day and diving hundreds of feet, are forced to live in confined spaces. Do you think they can get this type of exercise in a water tank? We don't think so.

Wait! There's more. Aquatic animals have a special way of talking to one another and finding their **prey**. They use sound patterns, or **echolocation**. This natural process is sometimes non-existent in aquariums because of the noise level and the glass enclosures. This type of confinement is unacceptable for any animal, anywhere.

The Born Free Foundation performed a worldwide study of zoos which revealed that zoochosis is rampant in confined animals around the globe. Another study found that elephants in zoos spend 22 percent of their time engaging in abnormal behaviors, such as repeated head bobbing or biting cage bars, and bears spend about 30 percent of their time pacing, a sign of distress.

Although zoos claim that their main purpose is to help prevent animals from becoming extinct and to help educate people about animals, we think the only thing zoos do is make animals crazy!

Captive Breeding and Reintroduction

"Zoos help animals survive and thrive."

—GERALDINE CURTATOLADO AND GARY QUAN

Zoos are a necessity to help preserve wildlife. Our world is filled with so many magnificent creatures: tigers, giant pandas, butterflies, to name a few. It's hard for us to believe that these animals are facing extinction. Why are so many animals in danger and what can be done to help them?

Zoos, wildlife centers, and refuge centers around the world are becoming involved in **captive breeding** programs. You might ask, *what is a captive breeding program?* It is the act of placing a male and a female of an endangered species together in a zoo, an aquarium, a wildlife center, or a refuge center in the hopes that they will reproduce. When babies are born, a population increases.

How does captive breeding work? To begin with, zookeepers and scientists from around the world work together to create a species survival plan. To put the plan together, the scientists gather as much information as possible about the species: for example, where the animals live, how far the animals move each day, what they eat, their habits, as well as the number of males and females that are left in the species.

If the number of animals in one species is very low, scientists may decide to capture all of the existing animals. Once they are captured,

giant panda

black-footed ferret

red wolf

bald eagle

male and female pairs of these animals are sent to different zoos. The zookeepers don't want to take a chance that disease or bad weather may wipe out the species before the animals begin to breed. This is what has been done with the red wolf, the black-footed ferret, and the bald eagle.

When the animals are settled, the breeding process begins. In 1970, forty red wolves were taken into captivity and sent to several zoos throughout the United States. Soon red cubs were born and their population began to increase.

In the late 1980s, there were only a few ferrets left in the wild. They were captured by zookeepers and put in a wildlife center in Wyoming. In 1987, seven baby ferrets were born. In 1988, 34 baby ferrets were born, and each year the number of births has grown.

The bald eagle, America's national symbol, was in great danger of becoming extinct. In 1782, when the eagle became our national symbol, there were between 25,000 and 75,000 eagles in the U.S. skies. Less than 3,000 were left in 1970. Captive breeding has brought back the bald eagle. In the early 1990s, there were more than 5,000 of them, and many more baby eagles are being born every day. It's great that our national symbol has survived!

"We are faced with stark alternatives; either we breed in captivity the ever increasing number of animal species threatened with extinction in the wild or they vanish forever." Zoos are here to help.

"Zoos help bring animals back into the wild."—GERALDINE AND GARY

Once the captive breeding programs have been successful in reproducing, the zookeepers and scientists must determine how to put the animals back into their natural habitats without the animals dying. This process is called **reintroduction**. It means scientists introduce these animals to places where they have not been in a long time.

Just like captive breeding, this is not an easy job. You cannot just pick up an animal, fly it 1,000 miles away, drop it off, and say, "Have a good life." Before an animal can be reintroduced to an area, the scientists need to learn everything they can about its natural habitat. It's also important to know as much as possible about the animal's habits.

Scientists must answer questions such as, how far is this animal accustomed to walking, running, flying, or swimming in a day? What types of food does the animal eat and how does it eat? When does this species have babies? Is there anything that could be harmful to the animal in this area? Will people accept the animal?

A zookeeper feeds a baby giraffe.

— 15 —

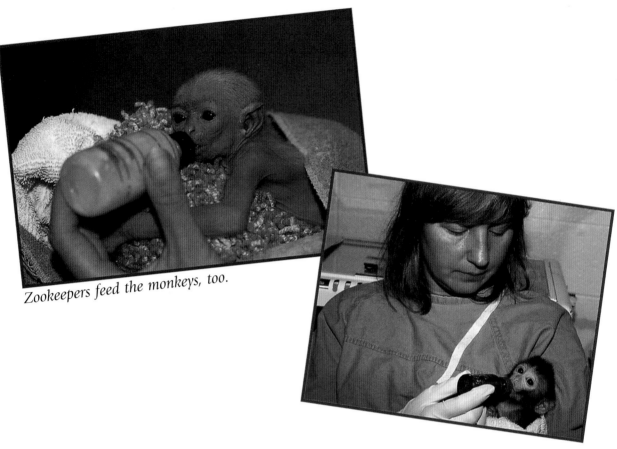

Zookeepers feed the monkeys, too.

As you can see, there are many questions to be answered before scientists can think about bringing an animal back to its natural habitat. If the conditions are not right, scientists might be causing more harm than good by reintroducing the animal.

After all the questions have been answered and the area chosen is determined to be a good one, the animals have to be taught how to be "wild." In captivity, these animals were protected and cared for by humans. To survive in the wild, they have to learn how to hunt for food, how to escape danger, and how to find shelter.

When scientists are sure the new habitat will meet all of the animal's needs and the animal has been taught to be wild, it is then time to set the animal free. Scientists and zookeepers work hard to reintroduce animals into their natural habitats.

Entertainment

"It's not normal for dolphins to jump through hoops for 'applause'."
—CHRISTIAN PAZUNO

Keeping animals in zoos to provide human entertainment—what a ludicrous idea! Don't you agree?

An aquarium is a type of zoo. Animals in aquariums are not kept in cages, but are kept in tanks filled with water. Research says that aquatic animals in the wild remain underwater for up to 30 minutes at a time and that they are used to spending 80 to 90 percent of their day underwater. In aquariums, the tanks that the animals live in are so shallow that captive orcas and dolphins spend more than half of their time at the surface. This can't possibly be good for these animals.

Think about it. We're kids and we are used to playing on the weekends and sometimes at night when our homework is finished. Imagine if we could only play for ten minutes a day. We wouldn't be happy, would we?

orca

bottlenose dolphins

sea lion

Animals kept in aquariums are forced to perform in three, four, or even five shows a day to entertain people. What do the animals get for this? A handful of fish? These animals must endure hard work and sometimes even pain to learn their tricks. In an article entitled "Captives of Cruelty," the authors state that "in order to learn tricks for their performances, these animals are subjected to abusive training. Some training methods used include beating the animal, using electric prods to shock the animal, and taking food away from the animal because it doesn't perform the tricks correctly."

I'm asking you to think of the suffering that these animals are forced to endure. I feel that attracting customers is the main business of a zoo. According to the People for Ethical Treatment of Animals (PETA), "Zoos are nothing more than animal prisons maintained for human amusement."

Death and Disease

"It is not the cages that really disturb us."
—ALLAN BARAHOMA AND CHRISTIAN PINTO

We say no to keeping animals in zoos! Animals in captivity are popular. Zoos, safari parks, wildlife centers, and aquariums are growing in number every single day.

But we are still against keeping animals in captivity. It is cruel to keep animals inside cages with no space to play. We believe animals have their right to freedom. Don't you?

Many animals have died in zoos because they are not well cared for. Some animals need to eat different types of foods that are found in their natural habitats. Sometimes it is difficult for zookeepers to get these foods, so they give the animals other things to eat. What if you were **diabetic,** and you couldn't find sugar-free foods to eat? Wouldn't you get sick after awhile?

Most animals in the wild are accustomed to hunting down their prey and eating constantly. An elephant, for example, can spend up to 20 hours a day searching for food. In a zoo, animals are put on

elephants

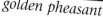
golden pheasant

orangutan

a feeding schedule. Depending on the zoo, animals are fed once or twice daily. This destroys their natural feeding patterns. Let's think about this for a moment. Most humans are used to eating three meals a day—breakfast, lunch, and dinner. What if you were told that you were no longer permitted to eat three times a day, but only once a day? Wouldn't you be hungry? Of course you would be.

There is a zoo where more than 30 animals died in a period of four months. Some of them included: parrots, eagles, pheasants, monkeys, deer, a chimpanzee, and an orangutan. These animals died because of these drastic changes to their lifestyle.

Disease is another problem. A baby elephant named Astor died in a zoo in 1983. Another baby elephant, Kumari, died in a zoo in 1995. An article written by Denise Grady states that both elephants died from a herpes **virus** which may be "...a direct result

of human meddling." Researchers think this virus is a major cause of death in Asian elephants that are kept in captivity.

Animals don't deserve this. Why are we putting them in a situation that will cause harm to them? We think animals should be kept out of zoos.

Research and Education

"Awareness is the key."—RONNY AND GUCCI

Without a doubt, animals should be kept in zoos. Keeping animals in a zoo means that scientists can study the animals and learn more about how a specific species lives, the type of foods the animals need, and their natural habits.

We feel that learning everything possible about an animal is the first step towards saving a species. It's easy to make bad decisions if we do not know enough.

bald eagle

A good example is our national symbol—the bald eagle. This majestic bird was once common throughout all of North America. Unfortunately, because of habitat loss, poison, and pollution within the food chain, bald eagles became endangered.

One of the reasons the bald eagle started to disappear was **DDT**. DDT is a pesticide, a chemical that is sprayed on crops by farmers to kill insects. As the eagles ate the food sprayed with this chemical, they began to get sick. The farmers didn't know this chemical would harm the eagle. All they wanted to do was save their crops.

What do you think would happen to you if you ate a poisonous chemical without knowing it? You might die. Well, let us tell you the harm this chemical has caused the bald eagle. When the eagles laid their eggs, the shells were very thin. Naturally, these eggs were very fragile. Most of them would crack before the baby eagles could hatch. The eagle population quickly decreased. The eagle became an endangered animal. Everyone was in a state of panic. How could we let this happen to our national symbol?

In 1972, after much research, scientists discovered that DDT was the problem. Farmers were no longer allowed to use this chemical. The bald eagle's population slowly began to increase. By raising the public's awareness, zoos helped to protect the entire species from extinction.

Additionally, zoos today try to educate their visitors by giving them information about the animals in them. Zoos do this in a

variety of ways. They publish guides about animals; they present movies and slide shows; and they display information. So we feel that zoos aid animals through research as well as by educating the public.

Natural Habitats

"Don't mess with nature!"—BISHOY AYOUB

The key to saving extinct animals lies in saving their habitats, not removing them from it only to be placed in an unnatural and abusive environment.

Animals need homes, just like people do. An animal's habitat is his or her home. It is the place where a particular species normally lives and thrives. An animal's habitat is special because it has all of the things an animal needs to live.

You might ask yourself, *What does an animal need to live?* Just like us, they need food, water, shelter, and a place to have their babies. Animals in the wild are accustomed to eating constantly and hunting for their food. In a zoo, this doesn't happen. Animals are also accustomed to moving about freely. For example, cheetahs are used to running and reaching speeds of 60 mph. In a zoo, animals don't have enough space to run that quickly. They'd crash into some type of barrier.

cheetah

Did you know that some animals rely on other animals? When one animal relies on another one for help, the two animals have a **symbiotic relationship**. Rhinoceroses and tick birds have this type of relationship. Here's how. A rhinoceros gets a lot of **ticks**. These ticks disturb the rhinoceros. The oxpecker, or tick bird, enjoys eating ticks, so it spends most of its life on the rhinoceros's back, removing the ticks and eating them. In zoos, it is not easy for animals to have these relationships.

symbiotic relationship of rhinoceros and tick bird

Removing an animal from its natural habitat can be detrimental to its health. It becomes very difficult for many animals to adapt to the constraints of a zoo. All of their natural habits are broken, causing illness or even death in some. So please, don't mess with nature!

Protection and Care

"Zoos are absolutely critical."—TORNEISHA CAMERON

Animals should be kept in zoos because they can receive better care and they are protected from their enemies.

In the wild, sometimes animals have a hard time finding food. In zoos, nutritionists work out menus for the animals and make sure they are fed every day. There is no danger of starvation.

In zoos, animals get the best veterinarian care. If they are sick or hurt, they will be treated quickly. Animals get vaccines which protect them against disease that can kill animals in the wild.

When animals are in the wild, they are in danger. There are no cages or enclosures to protect them from being hunted by other animals or even humans. In zoos, there is no danger of being hunted.

Scottish highlander being sprayed with water to keep cool

There are also different types of shelters in zoos to protect animals from harsh weather. Some zoos have sprinklers to cool off animals in the extreme heat!

Zoos even try to provide enrichment activities to help prevent boredom. One example of this is the chimpanzee termite mounds. Chimps in the wild come across large termite mounds. They jab them with sticks and lick the termites off, as though they were eating ice cream cones. In zoos, chimpanzees are given fake termite mounds with cool treats inside, like applesauce.

chimpanzee eating a "termite treat"

Why shouldn't animals stay in zoos? Which is better for an animal—to be protected or to die in the wild?

Should There Be Zoos?

Cast Your Vote

You have heard all of our arguments for zoos.

RONNY CALLE   GUCCI ATEHONTUA   GERALDINE CURTATOLADO   GARY QUAN   TORNEISHA CAMERON

You have heard all of our arguments against zoos.

STEPHANIE SANTANA   SHAUWN LUKOSE   CHRISTIAN PAZUNO   ALLAN BARAHOMA   CHRISTIAN PINTO   BISHOY AYOUB

It's time to tally your points and cast your vote.

Our Authors at Work

How We Wrote Our Persuasive Book

For eight weeks, we worked with our teachers, Ms. Ballester and Mr. Stead. We had been studying animals as a whole class and some of us thought it would be good to find out more about zoos and why they exist. We decided to write a persuasive book that looked at all of the positive and negative arguments about zoos. We thought that writing a persuasive book was going to be easy, but it wasn't.

We became really frustrated at times, but we kept on going. It was amazing to look at what we had written at the start and what we ended up with after all of our hard work. Here are the steps we took from beginning to end:

1. We listed all the issues that had to do with animals being kept in zoos and then selected the ones we thought were the most important.
2. We talked about the issues and started to form our opinions.
3. We listed all the arguments for and against keeping animals in zoos.
4. Each of us selected an issue that we felt strongly about.
5. We each took our key issue and formulated our arguments in writing.

6. We debated our issue and realized that we didn't have any facts to support our opinions. We also realized that some of our arguments were weak.

7. We researched. We went to the library and borrowed books on the issues, read articles, searched the Internet, and went on a field trip to a zoo. We learned so much.

8. After doing lots of reading, observing, and note-taking, we put our new information into our arguments to make them stronger. We constantly conferenced with our teachers.

9. We had many mini-lessons to help us improve our writing. Some of these lessons were: using opening quotes; learning ways to sustain our readers' attention; writing good beginnings and endings; using labels, illustrations, and pictures; and writing a glossary.

10. Finally, we read our finished arguments to each other, made a few changes, and then celebrated our writing. It was over, and we were proud of what we had done. We had learned so much about a persuasive text.

Glossary

aquarium	a zoo for animals that live in water
aquatic	living in, on, or near water
captive breeding	the act of putting males and females of the same species together to reproduce
captivity	to be kept against your own will
confinement	being closed in
DDT	a pesticide spray that is used to kill insects; it can kill humans and animals when it is swallowed or absorbed through the skin
diabetic	a disease in which increased sugar levels are found in the blood
echolocation	a method of using sound patterns that some animals use to find their prey
enclosure	a closed space
endangered	to be in danger, usually of becoming extinct
extinction	to be gone forever
food chain	a series of plants and animals in which each one is nourishment for the next one up the line
habitat	an animal's home
prey	food that an animal hunts
reintroduction	the process of putting animals that have been bred in captivity back into their natural habitats without the animals dying
species	animals and plants of one kind
symbiotic relationship	two different animals that live closely together often to the advantage of each of the animals
tick	a small, eight-legged animal that is related to spiders; ticks suck blood from the skin of animals and humans
virus	an illness
zoochosis	a kind of mental illness that animals kept in captivity can develop

Index